Old BULWELL

by
David Ottewell

The 'Bull Well', which is said to have given this area its name, is a small boggy area situated on Bestwood Road in what was originally part of Bulwell Forest. Some say the name is derived from the Saxon personal name 'Bulla', while others have suggested that 'bull' was an ancient word for the bubbling of water. The most picturesque explanation is that a bull gored a rock at this site and on pulling out his horn released a spring of water. The railway passed above this site just beyond the white fence.

© David Ottewell 2001
First published in the United Kingdom, 2001,
by Stenlake Publishing
Telephone / Fax: 01290 551122

ISBN 1 84033 154 2

FURTHER READING

The books listed below were used by the author during his research. None of them are available from Stenlake Publishing. Those interested in finding out more are advised to contact their local bookshop or reference library.

A. R. Griffin, *The Nottinghamshire Coalfield 1881–1981*, Moorland Publishing, 1981.

F. Hind et al, *Bulwell; Four Essays Towards a History of the Manor and Township*, Nottingham Corporation, 1948.

G. Jennings, *Bulwell and Basford on Old Postcards*, Reflections, 1993.

R. Mellors, *Old Nottingham Suburbs, Then and Now*, 1913.

R. Mellors, *The Gardens, Parks and Walks of Nottingham and District*, 1926.

St John's Church was designed by the architect William Knight and built on a site donated by Samuel Ball. The 6th Duke of Portland, who lived at Welbeck Abbey, travelled to Bulwell in 1882 to lay the foundation stone. The church was built in the Early English style, mainly using local Bulwell stone, and cost £5,000. Although it was opened in 1885 it was initially a chapel of ease within St Mary's parish, and did not acquire parish church status until 1928.

INTRODUCTION

Originally much of Nottinghamshire was wooded land interspersed with open spaces. The famous Sherwood Forest extended from Worksop in the north to the River Trent in the south. Bulwell lies four miles north-west of the city of Nottingham, and grew up on part of this tract of land. A natural, safe crossing point of the River Leen probably attracted the first settlers to the area; this is thought to have been in Saxon times.

One derivation of the name Bulwell is said to be from the Saxon personal name 'Bulla'. According to another theory it stems from the word 'bull', which translates as the bubbling sound made by running water.

In the Domesday survey, carried out in 1086 for William the Conqueror, Bulwell was assessed as comprising two carucates of land (about 240 acres) for tax purposes, of which one was farmed by a villein (a feudal tenant) and the other by a bordar (believed to be a tenant of a villein). The king granted the land to his follower William Peverel who became the first lord of the manor.

For hundreds of years Bulwell remained a small farming community, but gradually began to exploit the natural resources on which it stood, namely deposits of magnesian limestone, sandstone and coal. From the fifteenth century stone was quarried for use as building material, while limestone was extracted and processed to produce mortar and plaster.

The industrialisation of much of the country in the eighteenth century affected Bulwell and led to its growth. Stocking-frame knitting became a popular occupation in the district, and in a survey carried out in 1844 there were found to be 606 frames at work in the parish, mainly in individual homes. The growth of factories led to fears of unemployment and some outbreaks of Luddism. Another natural resource that was exploited was clay, which was extracted for use in the pottery industry where it was made into chimney pots, flower pots, bricks and terracotta decorations for buildings.

The presence of the River Leen encouraged the setting up of cotton mills to exploit its water power and by 1798 there were six operating in nearby Linby and Papplewick, where many Bulwell residents went to work. Both hosiery- and lace-making flourished in Nottinghamshire and the Leen valley provided a good area for setting up washing, bleaching and dyeing factories to finish these products.

Coal mining also made a large contribution to the rise of Bulwell. Cinderhill pit was sunk between 1841 and 1843, Hucknall in 1861 and Bestwood in 1872, all of which provided work for many men living in Bulwell. The arrival of the railways was another positive influence on Bulwell's development in the nineteenth century, with the Midland Railway being built through the town in 1848. This was followed by the Great Northern line in 1878 and the Great Central Company's line in 1895.

From a base of 1,585 in 1801, Bulwell's population grew to reach 4,276 by 1871. The last 30 years of the nineteenth century saw what can only be termed a population explosion, with a rise of over 10,000 resulting in a total of 14,767 residents being recorded in the 1901 census.

The town of Nottingham was also expanding in the second half of the nineteenth century and in 1877 Bulwell was brought into the Borough of Nottingham when Parliament passed the Nottingham Improvement and Borough Extension Act. Although it still has its own distinctive character, Bulwell is now very much a suburb of Nottingham.

THE LODGE, BULWELL HALL, NOTTS

TRAM TERMINUS, BULWELL, NOTTINGHAM.

In the early twentieth century the triangular Bulwell Market Place took up a relatively small area of land. The stalls were dismantled between markets, although the space was rarely used for other purposes. The row of buildings behind the market site has a plaque on it bearing the inscription 'H. G. H. 1883', which refers to the date it was erected and the original owner, George Harris, a local butcher. He employed Thomas Wright of Angel Row, Nottingham to come up with the design for him.

4

There appear to be no accurate records dating the start of the market in Bulwell, but it is thought to have originated around 1877 when Bulwell became part of Nottingham. This postcard dates from 1913 when the Maypole Dairy established a branch in Bulwell. The famous Nottingham company, Boots the Chemist, was also trading in Bulwell from a high-profile shop on the corner of Market Place and Main Street at this time. Local entrepreneur Jesse Boot had a policy of selling vast quantities of goods at a small profit per transaction, and for this he needed stores in prime positions that would attract a huge throughput of customers.

BULWELL MARKET PLACE.

A tram waiting to depart from Bulwell Market Place. Route No. 3 ran from here to Nottingham Market Place and then on to Trent Bridge. The vehicle featured in the picture has been adapted by the addition of a windscreen to offer the driver some protection from the elements – early trams had open cabs and open roofs. Businesses in the background include branches of the Westminster Bank and Maypole Dairy and Hickman's family butcher, reflecting a mixture of local and national businesses.

Market Square, Bulwell.

The arrival of trolleybuses in Bulwell on 13 May 1934 meant that the Market Place needed to be remodelled. Unlike trams which could be reversed at the end of their route, trolleybuses required space for turning round. The market site was made into an oval shape and when it was reopened by Alderman J. H. Freckingham in August 1934 it included electric lights and new covers for the stalls. The Olympia Theatre, on the left, opened in 1915, and from 1932 until its closure in 1952 it was called the Picture House.

QUARRY ROAD, BULWELL, NOTTINGHAM.

The building on the right of this picture of Quarry Road, faced with Bulwell stone, served as the reading room and public library until the 1920s when new, purpose-built premises were erected on Highbury Road. Writing in 1913, Robert Mellors said of the library: 'The accommodation provided for the purpose is very unsatisfactory and ought to be improved'. He noted that in 1912–1913 the estimated attendance in the reading room was 61,500, while the lending library had 19,761 visitors and the boys' and girls' library 11,938.

Quarry Road was renamed Commercial Road in 1913. Its original name reflected the presence of stone quarries in the area. As well as being used for building locally, Bulwell stone had a national reputation as a quality construction and paving material. Limestone was also quarried around Bulwell for burning to make mortar and plaster. This road was originally the site of Bulwell's pinfold.

Commercial Road, Bulwell. Rex Photo. 743.

Commercial Road leaves the Market Place from the north-west corner. Cunliffe's General Drapers stood on the corner of Pilkington Street, and the same premises are visible on page 9, where they were occupied by Eastman's Ltd. and were selling meat. A little further along the street is the Home and Colonial store, with Robinson's carriage works opposite.

Starr & Brookes' clothiers and jewellers store on Commercial Road at about the time of the First World War. Note the traditional pawnbroker's sign of three brass balls. In those days, with money tight, many working class families would have to resort to visiting 'Uncle' (as going to the pawnbroker's was sometimes referred to) to make ends meet. In 1913 there were six pawnbrokers in Bulwell.

A class from Commercial Road school in the early years of the twentieth century. It was generally standard practice to teach boys and girls separately. There appears to have been no uniform at this time.

Coventry Road in Edwardian times. The extensive shop premises on the left, with the large display of dresses and other clothing outside, belonged to the Midland Drapery Company. Note the stepladder, which would have been essential for reaching articles for customers.

Strelley House, Bulwell. No. 3330.

Strelley House was built by George Strelley, who was Mayor of Plymouth and the son of John Strelley of Hempshill. It was constructed in 1677 as a free school for local boys. Prior to this they had to travel to Nuthall for education. Originally Strelley House was quite a small structure comprising a school room and master's house. Later it was extended on the northern side and a porch was added. It was constructed on a base of hammer-dressed Bulwell stone using irregular bricks. The later porch incorporates a carved stone panel featuring the Strelley coat of arms in the centre. The last schoolmaster was Joseph Calladine who served for 44 years. He died in 1866 and the school declined after his death, closing in 1885. In 1916 Harry Gill restored the building and converted it into a private residence.

Looking south-west down Main Street into Market Place. To the left is Hilton's boot and shoe shop. In the distance is the distinctive tower of the Wesleyan chapel, in front of which was G. Blewett's herbalists.

The buildings on the right of this picture of Main Street have long since been demolished. A little further up on this, the north side of Main Street, was another of Bulwell's cinemas, the Palace, which was owned by Edwin Widdowson. A pair of public houses, the Golden Ball and the Royal Oak, stand side by side on the left-hand side. At the start of the First World War there were 22 public houses in Bulwell.

An impressive turnout of the Bulwell Salvation Army band. From 1908 the Salvation Army had their own hall on Main Street. There is only one female among the thirty individuals gathered in the band. This is an appropriate picture in a book about a Nottingham suburb as the founder of the Salvation Army, William Booth, was born at 12 Notingtone Place in Sneinton, Nottingham, on 10 April 1829. Although he left for London in 1849 and founded the Salvation Army there, he never forgot his humble beginnings as the third of five children in a poor family, serving as an apprentice to a pawnbroker in his home town.

Main Street
Bulwell.
Rex Photo. 3857

Ironically, one of Bulwell's numerous pubs, the Scots Grey, can be seen just beyond the Salvation Army hall (built 1908). The hall is the church-like building in the foreground, and the Scots Grey is the ornate stone-fronted building beyond it. A fixture in Bulwell for many years, the Scots Grey was rebuilt in brick in 1884, leaving the remains of a much older stone building behind it.

The Leen, an important tributary of the River Trent, rises in Kirkby Forest before travelling a little over 14 miles to join the Trent near Nottingham. Part of its course is through Bulwell. Unfortunately it is prone to flooding in this area and Bulwell has suffered on a number of occasions. This postcard, sent from Bulwell in 1908, shows a flooded Main Street at its junction with Minerva Street. A number of children have removed their shoes and socks to paddle in what must have been very dirty water.

1932 was also a bad year for flooding. Bexton's fish and chip shop was among the many businesses cut off by floods – which appear to be up to a foot deep in these photographs.

The National School, at the bottom of Ragdale Road, was built in 1866 on an area of land known as Bulwell Green. It had been one of the few unenclosed areas of land in Bulwell, and many people were opposed to the use of the site for building, as they viewed it as an example of the wealthy depriving the poor of one of the few amenities they had. This still rankled 50 years later when Robert Mellors wrote in 1913 that: 'It would have been better had they left the Green as an open space and built the school on another site'. The building, including a master's house, cost £3,000, and when completed the school had room for 518 pupils.

Main Street, Bulwell. No. 254.

The horse and cart, with its two bowler-hatted occupants, is making its way out of Bulwell towards Hucknall Lane. The cottages across the road in the middle distance were demolished to make way for the Adelphi Cinema; an extremely popular entertainment centre designed by Reginald W. Cooper of Nottingham and built in 1937–1938 in the art deco style. Failing attendances meant that it closed as a cinema in 1963, although it enjoyed a long life after that as a bingo hall.

Main Street, Bulwell, Nottingham.

Peveril Series. 3

Just beyond the school on the corner of Main Street and Ragdale Road is the Methodist chapel, the foundation stones for which were laid in August 1882. The design of the building was unusual, with the chapel on the first floor and the ground floor taken up with schoolrooms.

The 26-arch viaduct on Hucknall Lane was a familiar feature of local life until it was demolished in more recent times. The 420 yard long structure involved the use of 6.5 million bricks and took twelve months to built. It carried the Great Central Railway over the Leen Valley.

Bestwood, Iron Works. 625. Spree.

Bestwood Colliery was sunk in 1871–1872 by the Lancaster family of Lancashire. It remained in production until 1967. The largest landowner in Bestwood, the Duke of St Albans, set up an ironworks in the village (above) which began operations in 1877 and ceased production in 1928. The importance of these two industries to the neighbouring village of Bulwell is highlighted by Robert Mellors, who notes that: 'The sinking of Bestwood Pit and afterwards the formation of the iron smelting works had a very material bearing in Bulwell because of the large number of men employed there but residing in Bulwell.' Taking into account this pit and other local ones, it is estimated that at the turn of the twentieth century up to two thirds of local families were involved in mining in some way.

The area of scrubland situated between the villages of Bulwell and Bestwood and known as Bulwell Forest was turned into a public park in 1877. Ten years later the Notts. Golf Club laid out a 7 hole golf course on part of the forest lands, although it wasn't until 1894 that they managed to extend it to the traditional 18 holes. In 1900 the club took the decision to move their home to Holinwell.

After the transfer of the Notts. Golf Club from Bulwell Forest in 1900, three new clubs made it their home course. The Bulwell Forest Club was founded in 1902 and was joined by Bulwell Artisans Golf Club and the St Albans Ladies Golf Club.

LADIES' PAVILION, BULWELL GOLF LINKS, NOTTINGHAM.

The main pavilion cost £8,447 to erect, and local historian Robert Mellors described it thus: 'There is a well appointed pavilion and dressing rooms with 504 lockers, a dining and smoke room and comfortable quarters for the stewards and refreshments are supplied at very reasonable prices.'

GOLF PAVILION, BULWELL, NOTTINGHAM.

27

Squire's Lane was originally a rough track used by local farmers. However, when the Rev. Padley acquired Bulwell Hall and the status of lord of the manor in November 1820, he set about landscaping the area, planting trees in what became Bulwell Wood and laying out the grounds of the hall. He also widened Squire's Lane, planted young trees by its side and put a gravel surface on the road to form a carriage drive to his residence. Part of the land flanking the lane was built on in the 1920s, while the bottom section was used for housing in 1957.

For many years the grounds of Bulwell Hall were the venue for the Church School annual tea party, held in autumn. Children would arrive on the allotted day in their Sunday best and collect windfall apples in the orchard before being served tea by their teachers and volunteers from the elite of Bulwell society. Afterwards games were organised in the spacious grounds.

Bulwell Hall Park. No. 265

The lodge gates of Bulwell Hall in Squire's Lane. Another event on the estate was 'Cowslip Sunday'. A field surrounded by an iron fence was covered each year in cowslips, and a day was set aside on which crowds were allowed to enter the field and gather armfuls of the yellow blooms.

Bulwell Hall was built in 1770 by John Newton and was initially known as Pye-Wip Hall. When Newton died in 1820 ownership of the hall passed to his son, Robert, who only survived his father by twelve days. By this means the Rev. Alfred Padley, the grandson of John Newton, unexpectedly acquired the hall. He set about enlarging Bulwell Hall and improving the grounds.

After the Rev. Padley died on 11 May 1856 the hall passed through the hands of various owners including Thomas Hardy of Kimberley, one of the brothers who founded the famous brewery there. On his death it was sold to Sir Albert Ball. He was the father of the famous First World War aviator, also called Albert, who shot down 44 enemy planes but was tragically killed aged only 20, and was posthumously awarded the Victoria Cross. Sir Albert eventually sold the hall to Nottingham Corporation for £35,000. They used it as a residential sanatorium for tuberculosis suffers.

Flower Garden, Bulwell Hall, Notts.

In the 1930s the corporation had plans to turn Bulwell Hall into an approved school but these were dropped when the army requisitioned it from 1939 to 1947. At the end of the war it stood unoccupied and fell into a poor state of repair until it was demolished in the 1960s. It is claimed that the clock, on the tower to the right, stood forlornly at seven o'clock for many years.

Many events took place in the spacious, well appointed grounds of Bulwell Hall. This postcard was published to celebrate a balloon ascent from the grounds. It was sent in December 1906, but unfortunately the local papers for that period reveal nothing about the flight. In 1897 local children were invited up to Bulwell Hall where they were presented with a new penny to celebrate Queen Victoria's Diamond Jubilee.

BALOON ASCENT.

BULWELL HALL, NOTTINGHAM.

Bulwell Hall golf course was opened on 26 May 1910. It had 18 holes and covered over 6,000 yards. A pavilion (above) was built at the entrance to the hall's parkland, adjoining the Great Central Railway's Bulwell Hall Halt station. Nottingham City Golf Club had their headquarters here. Initially season tickets were two guineas for gentlemen and one and a half guineas for ladies.

This photograph was taken from the bridge over the River Leen looking towards Cinderhill. The solitary house on the left is called Riverlyn but was once known as Horse Shoe Cottage. A date stone on the porch indicates that it was built in 1868. Today it is a health centre. The area pictured here was known as 'The Bogs' and was a favourite play area for local children. However in 1868 S. T. Cooper, the then lord of the manor, fenced it off much to the annoyance of locals. The ensuing dispute became known as The Battle of the Bog. Eventually Nottingham Corporation stepped in to mediate, bought the land and reopened it as a playground.

The bridge spanning the River Leen, which provides access from the Market Place to the station area, has a date stone of 1837 but is thought to have been built four years earlier. The carved initials on the bridge, G. H., refer to George Holmes, the builder. Rev. Padley gave £200 towards the cost of the bridge's construction. It was close to this site that the village stocks were sited, and local punishments were carried out here until the practice was abolished in 1875. The Leen played an important part in the economy of Bulwell. At one stage it provided power to a number of cotton mills in the area, and it was also important for the washing, bleaching and dyeing undertaken by Bulwell firms on behalf of hosiery and lace companies. The Leen also had a malevolent side, however, often flooding. In 1873 for instance, thirteen people died in the floods caused when it burst its banks.

An early open-topped tram waiting at the terminus in Bulwell prior to setting off on its journey to Trent Bridge via Nottingham Market Place. The Bulwell route was the second to open on the Nottingham system, demonstrating the importance of the area. The first tram ran on 23 July 1901, and the fare to Nottingham was 3d. Trams were soon adapted with the addition of roofs to protect passengers on the upper deck from the elements.

MIDLAND STATION, BULWELL. NOTTINGHAM.

The Midland Railway's station at Bulwell was built using local stone. The station, seen here looking north, was constructed on a site overlooking the area known as The Bogs. It was called Bulwell Market to differentiate it from the three other local stations: Bulwell Common, Bulwell Forest and Bulwell Hall Halt. The station came into operation on 2 October 1848 and provided an efficient service: for instance in 1948 it took 17 minutes to travel between Bulwell and Nottingham and the cheapest fare was only 5½d. The last passenger train ran on 12 October 1964 to Mansfield; goods services continued to use the line until 7 August 1967. Since 1994 the station has received a new lease of life as part of the Robin Hood Line, on which trains operate from Nottingham to Worksop via Mansfield.

Free Library & Church Bulwell. Rex Photo 3850.

A pair of Nottingham Corporation trolleybuses passing each other near Bulwell library. Trolleybuses, which were known affectionately as 'tracklesses', operated on the route to Nottingham from 13 May 1934 after the withdrawal of the trams. They in turn were replaced by buses in 1965. The impressive library was opened in 1923 and still serves the community today.

This postcard of Highbury Vale, sent from Bulwell in September 1910, demonstrates that in Edwardian times there were still few motor vehicles in use and that horse-drawn transport, supplemented by trams, was the order of the day. The ornate posts carrying the overhead tram wires were a prominent item of street furniture at the time. Most of Highbury Vale was built in the last twenty years of the nineteenth century to provide accommodation for Bulwell's ever-increasing population. The building with the bay window is Ebenezer Cottage and dates from 1890.

Towards the end of the nineteenth century Highbury Road replaced Station Road as the main thoroughfare out of Bulwell towards Nottingham. After climbing the hill from the Market Place and passing St Mary's Church, the Highbury Vale Hotel (right) was reached.

As Highbury Vale was some distance from the centre of Bulwell, it became necessary to build facilities for the area's large population; these included shops, the Northern Baths, and the Henry Mellish School. Highbury Vale post office was situated in the nearest shop in the three-storey terrace. Just beyond the shops is the turning into Broomhill Road.

Vernon Road, Basford. No. 26

Vernon Road was an extension of Highbury Road and led directly to the centre of Bulwell. In this 1920s' view tramcar No. 165 is on route 3 from Nottingham to Bulwell. This was a period of transition in road transport. Motorised vehicles, like the three-wheeled car parked outside the shops, were becoming an increasingly familiar sight, although horse-drawn delivery vehicles were still plentiful.

As the main open space in the centre of Bulwell, the Market Place was not only the venue for weekly markets, but gatherings of both a religious and secular nature. Here a service is being held, probably to dedicate Bulwell's memorial to those who lost their lives in the First World War, in front of a substantial crowd of onlookers, many of whom are in uniform.

Bulwell Wakes was an event looked forward to by many locals. Although not on the same scale as the annual Goose Fair in Nottingham, it nevertheless attracted large crowds. Wagons carrying rides and sideshows arrived in Bulwell pulled by steam traction engines or horses, and the showmen set up on the Market Place or down by the River Leen. There would be rides like the gallopers and roundabouts, and stalls such as the coconut shy. Other attractions included sideshows where visitors could pay to see exotic people or wild animals.

The cemetery at Bulwell was laid out on 18 acres of land by the Public Parks and Burial Committee in 1903. The cost including the offices and necessary improvements to Hempshill Lane was £10,130.

CEMETERY GATES & OFFICES
BULWELL, NOTTM.

PEVERIL SERIES No 367.

Northern Cemetery, Bulwell. No. 3331.

Bulwell's new cemetery included a Gothic-style chapel. Writing in 1926, Robert Mellors described the cemetery in terms more suited to a public park, observing: 'The air is bracing, the views extensive and there are comfortable seats.'

43

HEMPSHILL FAN

Thomas North was a nineteenth century coal mining entrepreneur who set up a number of pits in the area including Cinderhill, Babbington, Newcastle, Broxtowe and Kimberley. Collectively they were known as the Babbington group. The first deep mine was Cinderhill, sunk between 1841 and 1843. North started work on Bulwell Pit in 1867 but before he could complete it he died, and it was bought into full production by Wright and Co. in 1869. Hempshill Fan, situated near Hempshill Lane, was linked to both Babbington and Bulwell collieries and provided a vital ventilation shaft for both pits. There was a major fire in the shaft in August 1935 which was thought to have been caused by a spark from a train passing on the nearby Nottingham to Ilkeston branch line.

An early, solid-tyred bus registered AU 2162 belonging to A. Lowe of 24 Strelley Street, Bulwell. Although Nottingham Corporation provided a tram service into Nottingham from 1901, and replaced it with a trolleybus service in the 1930s, there was still room for local initiative. Few people owned their own cars and there was a demand for transport both to work and on pleasure outings. Mr Lowe is seen here posing with his bus, which offered 'The Elite' service.

The first Wesleyan church in Bulwell was built in 1811 and was replaced by this building, which cost £3,500, in 1882. It is also visible in the picture on page 15, and its site is now occupied by the bus station.

St Mary's Church was designed by H. T. Stevens of Derby and built in 1850 in what was described as 'fourteenth century Decorated style'. A great deal of Bulwell stone was used in its construction. It replaced a smaller church with medieval origins that had been reconstructed in the eighteenth century and was sited about 40 yards further north. The presence of an earlier church on the site explains why there are some graves in the churchyard that predate the building of St Mary's. Chief amongst these is that of George Robinson (died 1790), famous for setting up a string of cotton mills on the River Leen towards Papplewick.

Market Place, Bulwell. Nott™. 630. Spree.

Bulwell Market Place in the mid-1920s. At the time trams still left from the terminus here, although the service was reaching the end of its active life. The building on the corner of Main Street and Highbury Road carries a plethora of advertisements, including one for locally-produced Players Navy Cut. The introduction of the tram service had meant that more Bulwell residents could travel into Nottingham to work at factories like Players and Raleigh, which were both expanding in the early years of the twentieth century.

MARKET PLACE, BULWELL, NOTTINGHAM.

The Market Place was the most popular subject for local producers of postcards, for not only was it easy to get a tram in the picture (with arrivals and departures approximately every five minutes), but there tended to be people about in what was the main shopping area. This picture dates from shortly after 1900.